The new Solar System

Robin Birch

The Moon

CHELSEA
CLUBHOUSE
An Imprint of Chelsea House Publishers

Chelsea Clubhouse
An imprint of Chelsea House Publishers
132 West 31st Street
New York, NY 10001

Chelsea Clubhouse books are available at special discounts when purchased in bulk quantities for businesses, associations, institutions, or sales promotions. Please call our Special Sales Department in New York at (212) 967-8800 or (800) 322-8755.

You can find Chelsea Clubhouse on the World Wide Web at: http://www.chelseahouse.com

First published in 2004 by
MACMILLAN EDUCATION AUSTRALIA PTY LTD
15–19 Claremont Street, South Yarra, 3141

Visit our Web site at www.macmillan.com.au or go directly to www.macmillanlibrary.com.au

Associated companies and representatives throughout the world.

Copyright © Robin Birch 2004

Library of Congress Cataloging-in-Publication Data

Birch, Robin.
    The moon / Robin Birch. — 2nd ed.
    p. cm. — (The new solar system)
    Includes index.
    ISBN 978-1-60413-207-6
    1. Moon—Juvenile literature. I. Title.
    QB582.B57 2008
    523.3—dc22

                                    2007051541

Edited by Anna Fern
Text and cover design by Cristina Neri, Canary Graphic Design
Photo research by Legend Images
Illustrations by Melissa Webb, Noisypics

Printed in the United States of America

Acknowledgements

The author and publisher are grateful to the following for permission to reproduce copyright material:

Cover photograph of the Moon courtesy of Digital Vision.

Bruce Davidson—OSF/Auscape, p. 4; Reg Morrison/Auscape, p. 16 (right); Richard Packwood—OSF/Auscape, p. 22 (bottom); Biblioteca Nazionale-Florence, Italy, p. 24; Australian Picture Library/Corbis, pp. 9, 13 (right); Digital Vision, pp. 5, 23 (right); Calvin J. Hamilton, pp. 7, 10; Marie Lochman/Lochman Transparencies, pp. 17, 20; Walter Myers/www.arcadiastreet.com, p. 8; NASA/Human Space Flight, pp. 27, 29; NASA/Kennedy Space Center, pp. 25, 26; NASA/NSSDC, p. 13 (left); NASA/US Geological Survey, p. 15; Photodisc, pp. 14, 16 (left); Photolibrary.com/SPL, pp. 6, 28.

Background and border images courtesy of Photodisc, and view of the Moon courtesy of Digital Vision.

While every care has been taken to trace and acknowledge copyright, the publisher offers their apologies for any accidental infringement where copyright has proved untraceable. Where the attempt has been unsuccessful, the publisher welcomes information that would redress the situation.

Please note

At the time of printing, the Internet addresses appearing in this book were correct. Owing to the dynamic nature of the Internet, however, we cannot guarantee that all these addresses will remain correct.

Contents

Glossary words

When you see a word printed in bold, **like this**, you can look up its meaning in the glossary on page 31.

Discovering the Moon

The Moon is the brightest object in the sky, after the Sun. Moonlight at night is sometimes so bright that some people can read by it.

The Moon has gray patches surrounded by bright silvery areas. In 1609, the **astronomer** Galileo Galilei studied the Moon with a **telescope** and saw that the gray patches looked like flat seas. He called them *"maria,"* which is Latin for "seas." We now know that the maria are flat, gray plains, and the silver parts are mountain areas.

▼ The Moon

The **ancient** Romans called the Moon *"Luna."* Today we use the word "lunar" to describe things having to do with the Moon.

The word "month" comes from "Moon," probably because there is usually one full moon every month.

▲ This is the symbol for the Moon.

The Moon is 238,700 miles
(384,400 kilometers) from Earth.

▶ An astronaut
on the Moon

The same side of the Moon always faces Earth, so the other side of the Moon was not discovered for a long time. In 1959, the **space probe** *Luna 3* circled the Moon and took pictures of the back of the Moon.

In 1968, **astronauts** flew around the Moon for the first time. The first Moon landing was in 1969. Since then five more crews of astronauts have walked on the Moon, the last in 1972. On the last three trips, astronauts used a moon buggy to explore the area around their landing site.

The Moon and the Solar System

The Moon **orbits** the **planet** Earth. The planet Earth **revolves** around the Sun, along with seven other planets and many other bodies. The Sun, planets, and other bodies together are called the solar system.

The solar system has eight planets. Mercury, Venus, Earth, and Mars are made of rock. They are the smallest planets, and are closest to the Sun. Jupiter, Saturn, Uranus, and Neptune are made mainly of **gas** and liquid. They are the largest planets.

The solar system also has dwarf planets. The first three bodies to be called dwarf planets were Ceres, Pluto, and Eris. Ceres is an asteroid. Pluto and Eris are known as **trans-Neptunian objects**.

Most planets and dwarf planets in the solar system have one or more **moons**. They stay in their orbits because the planets' **gravity** holds them in place.

A planet is a body that:
- orbits the Sun
- is nearly round in shape
- has cleared the area around its orbit (its gravity is strong enough)

A dwarf planet is a body that:
- orbits the Sun
- is nearly round in shape
- has not cleared the area around its orbit
- is not a moon

▲ The solar system

There are also many small solar system bodies in the solar system. These include asteroids, comets, trans-Neptunian objects, and other small bodies which have not been called dwarf planets.

Asteroids are made of rock. Most of them, including dwarf planet Ceres, orbit the Sun in a path called the asteroid belt. The asteroid belt lies between the orbits of Mars and Jupiter. Comets are made mainly of ice and rock. When their orbits bring them close to the Sun, comets grow a tail. Trans-Neptunian objects are icy, and orbit the Sun farther out on average than Neptune.

▶ The eight planets are Mercury, Venus, Earth, Mars, Jupiter, Saturn, Uranus, and Neptune.

The solar system is about 4,600 million years old.

The name "solar system" comes from the word "Sol," the Latin name for the Sun.

Planet	Average distance from Sun	
Mercury	35,960,000 miles	(57,910,000 kilometers)
Venus	67,190,000 miles	(108,200,000 kilometers)
Earth	92,900,000 miles	(149,600,000 kilometers)
Mars	141,550,000 miles	(227,940,000 kilometers)
Jupiter	483,340,000 miles	(778,330,000 kilometers)
Saturn	887,660,000 miles	(1,429,400,000 kilometers)
Uranus	1,782,880,000 miles	(2,870,990,000 kilometers)
Neptune	2,796,000,000 miles	(4,504,000,000 kilometers)

On the Moon

As it travels around Earth, the Moon spins on its **axis**. The airless, lifeless Moon is very different from Earth.

Size and Structure

The Moon is 2,159 miles (3,476 kilometers) in **diameter**. It is a little less than one-third as wide as Earth.

Gravity is six times weaker on the Moon than it is on Earth. This is because the Moon is smaller than Earth, and has a lower **density**. A person on the Moon can jump higher more easily than they can on Earth, because they are not as heavy as they are on Earth.

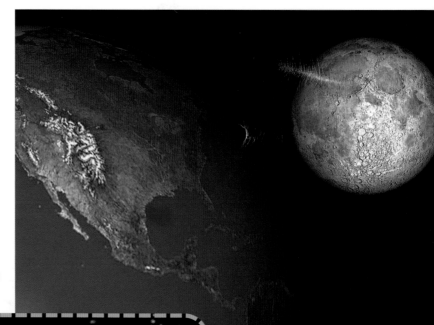

▶ Compare the size of the Moon and Earth.

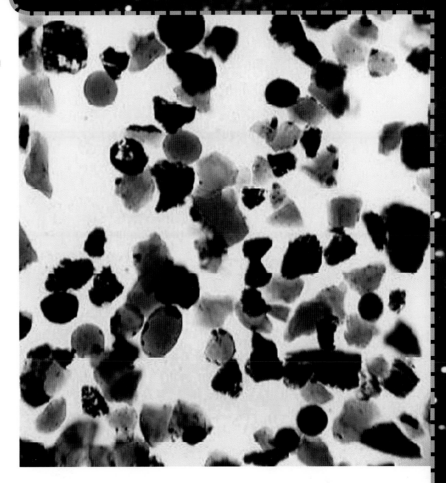

▶ Orange soil from the Moon

Crust

The outside layer of the Moon is called the crust. The Moon's crust is made of hardened rocks with soil on them. The crust is about 60 miles (100 kilometers) thick in some places, and almost nothing in others. It is thinner on the side of the Moon which faces Earth. The crust was hot and **molten** when the Moon was young, and cooled to become solid about 4,400 million years ago.

The soil on the Moon is called regolith. The regolith has been formed by asteroids hitting the Moon and breaking the rock up into tiny particles. Many soil particles have melted and turned into tiny orange glass beads.

Mantle and Core

Below its crust, the Moon has a **mantle** made of rock. The rock is probably partly solid and partly liquid. The Moon probably has a small **core** in the middle. The core does not appear to contain the metal iron, like Earth's core.

There seems to be no activity going on inside the Moon, and there are no active **volcanoes**. Astronauts left instruments behind on the Moon to measure moonquakes, but very little movement has been detected.

▼ Inside the Moon

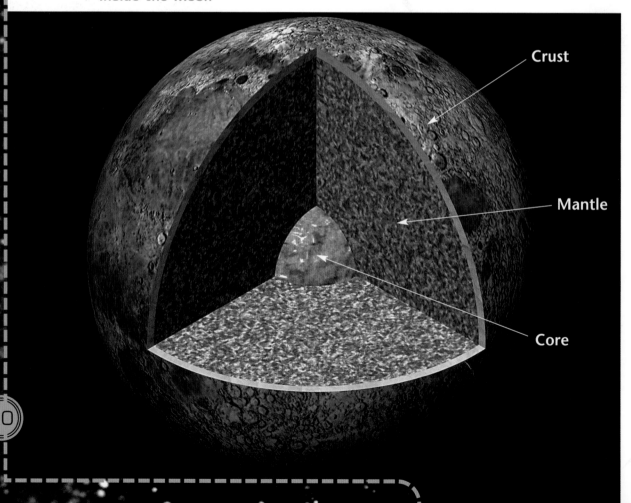

Crust

Mantle

Core

1. Large object slams into Earth.

2. Ring of broken rock forms around Earth.

3. Rocks form a ball—the Moon.

▲ The formation of the Moon

Moon's Formation

The Moon probably formed after an object the size of Mars hit Earth really hard. The object would have broken a lot of rock off the outside layer of Earth, leaving the inside part of Earth untouched. The broken rock would have formed a ring around Earth and, eventually, the flying rock would have been pulled into one ball, which became the Moon.

This idea about the Moon's formation explains why the Moon does not have an iron core like Earth. It would have been made of lightweight rocks from the outer layer of Earth.

11

Highlands and Plains

The Moon is bright silver-white, with darker gray patches. The bright areas are the highlands, which consist of mountains, hills, and valleys. They are covered with **craters**. The highlands are very old. They were formed when the Moon formed, 4,600 million years ago.

The dark patches on the Moon are called *"maria,"* which is Latin for "seas." They looked like flat seas to the first astronomers who studied them closely. The seas are plains made from **lava** which flowed into large impact craters and hardened. They are fairly smooth and are younger than the highlands. The seas have some small **volcanic** craters on them, and some long trenches called rilles.

▼ Map of the Moon

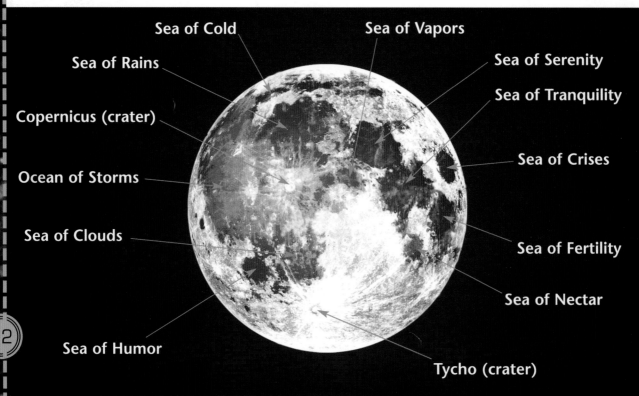

Sea of Cold

Sea of Vapors

Sea of Rains

Sea of Serenity

Sea of Tranquility

Copernicus (crater)

Ocean of Storms

Sea of Crises

Sea of Clouds

Sea of Fertility

Sea of Nectar

Sea of Humor

Tycho (crater)

▼ The far side of the Moon is on the left of this picture. The small sea in the middle is called Orientale. The large basin on the lower left is South Pole-Aitken.

▲ The *Apollo 14* mission exploring on the side of the Moon that faces away from Earth

There are 11 major seas on the side of the Moon which faces Earth and only one major sea on the side of the Moon which faces away from Earth. This may be because the Moon's crust is thinner on the side of the Moon which faces Earth. Then lava could have gotten through the crust more easily, from the mantle below.

Volcanoes stopped gushing lava into the seas about 2,000 million years ago. By this time, the rock made from cooled lava was so thick that it prevented more lava from coming up.

Craters

Impact craters formed on the Moon when asteroids hit it. Most of the impact craters were made more than 3,000 million years ago, as this was when there were a lot of asteroids flying around in the solar system.

The Moon's largest crater, and the largest impact crater in the solar system, is South Pole-Aitken. It is on the far side of the Moon. Some craters have mountains in the middle of them. Some have pale rays coming from them, like spokes. The rays are made from dust thrown up when the asteroid hit. The large rayed crater Tycho is easy to see with **binoculars**.

▼ The crater Copernicus is about 56 miles (90 kilometers) in diameter, and has long rays coming from it. It has tall walls and a flat floor with mountains in the middle.

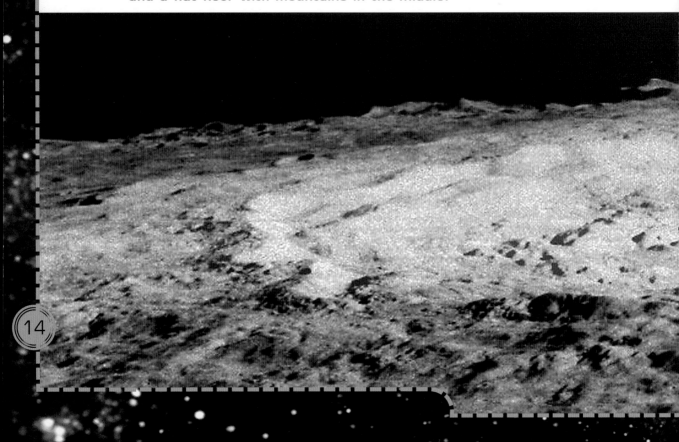

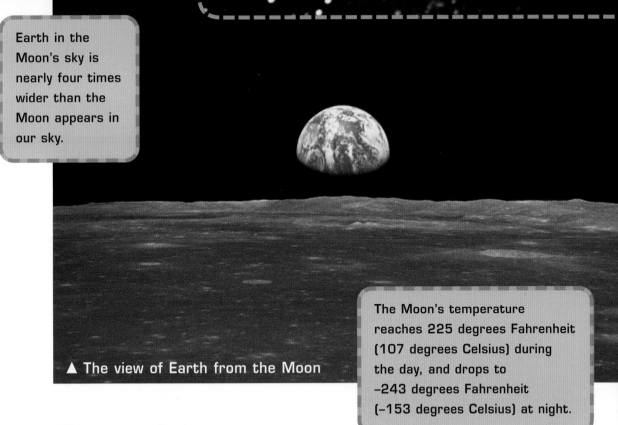

Earth in the Moon's sky is nearly four times wider than the Moon appears in our sky.

The Moon's temperature reaches 225 degrees Fahrenheit (107 degrees Celsius) during the day, and drops to −243 degrees Fahrenheit (−153 degrees Celsius) at night.

▲ The view of Earth from the Moon

Atmosphere

The Moon has no **atmosphere** and no liquid water on it. This means there has been no weather to wear away the craters, like there has been on Earth.

The space probe *Lunar Prospector* has found there is probably water ice at the Moon's north and south **poles**. This ice may be deep in craters, where sunshine cannot reach it. The ice would have come from comets which have crashed into the Moon.

The sky on the Moon is black, because there is no atmosphere. From the Moon, the Sun is a round, bright object, shining in a black sky. The stars are tiny bright dots which do not twinkle.

There is no atmosphere, so there is no sound on the Moon, because sound is carried by substances such as air.

The Moon from Earth

The Moon orbits around Earth in 27.3 days. The Moon always has the same side facing Earth, so the pattern of seas and highlands on the Moon always looks the same. This is because, as it orbits, the Moon also rotates on its axis once every 27.3 Earth days. Humans did not see the far side of the Moon until the space probe *Luna 3* took photographs of it, in 1959.

The Moon appears upside-down to people in the Southern **Hemisphere**, compared to the way people in the Northern Hemisphere see it. This is because people in the north and south are looking at the Moon from different directions.

▼ The Moon from the United States, in the Northern Hemisphere

▼ The Moon from Australia, in the Southern Hemisphere

▲ Moon rise

The Moon is in the daytime sky just as often as it is in the night sky. However, we cannot see it during the day when it is close to the Sun.

The Moon rises about 50 minutes later each day. It rises in the east and sets in the west. We see the Moon moving through the sky because Earth is spinning. When the Moon is rising, it seems very large, but it is really no larger than when it is high in the sky.

The Moon shines brightly when it is in the night sky because it is lit up by the Sun shining on it. The Moon reflects sunlight back to Earth, making moonlight. The Moon can often be seen easily during the day, but it does not seem as bright then because the sky around it is lit up.

Phases

The Moon appears to change shape over a month-long period. These shapes are called phases. They are caused by the Moon revolving around Earth. The bright part of the Moon is having daytime, and the dark part of the Moon is having nighttime. All parts of the Moon have day and night.

When the Moon comes between Earth and the Sun, the side of the Moon facing Earth is dark. This is called a new moon. The Moon does not usually block out the Sun because the Sun and Moon do not usually line up exactly.

▼ Why the Moon has phases

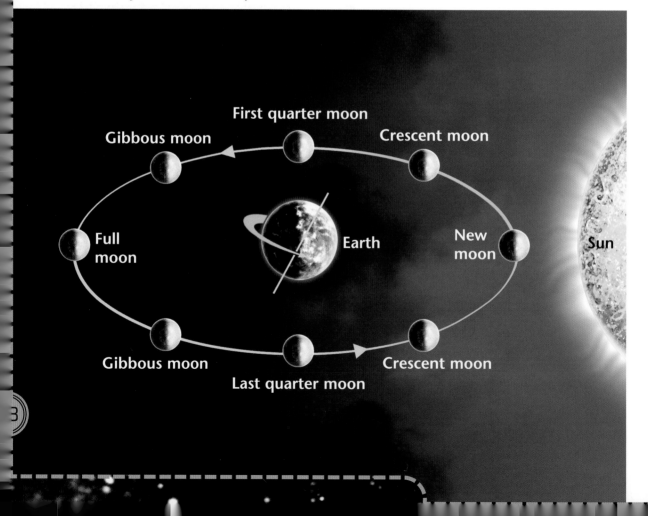

First quarter moon

Gibbous moon

Crescent moon

Full moon

Earth

New moon

Sun

Gibbous moon

Last quarter moon

Crescent moon

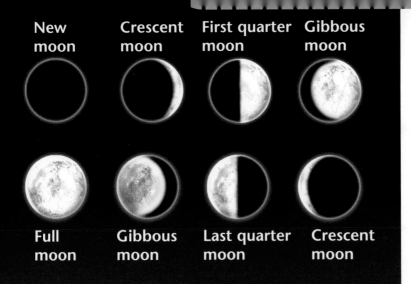

New moon Crescent moon First quarter moon Gibbous moon

Full moon Gibbous moon Last quarter moon Crescent moon

▲ Moon's phases, seen from the Northern Hemisphere

▼ Moon's phases, seen from the Southern Hemisphere

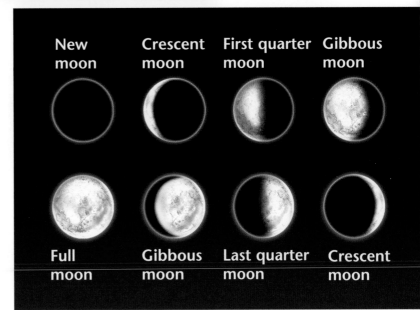

New moon Crescent moon First quarter moon Gibbous moon

Full moon Gibbous moon Last quarter moon Crescent moon

When the Moon is on the opposite side of Earth from the Sun, the Sun shines on the side of the Moon facing Earth. This is called a full moon. When the Moon is half-way between new moon and full moon, the Sun shines on half of the side of the Moon facing Earth. These two positions make the first quarter moon and the last quarter moon. It takes 29.5 days for the Moon to pass from one new moon to the next.

The Moon Lit Up

Full moons in different months have been given names by Native Americans and the first European settlers in America. They called the September full moon a "harvest moon," and the October full moon a "hunter's moon."

When there are two full moons in the same month, the second one is called a "blue moon."

When the Moon is less than full, we can see the dark part of the Moon against the sky. This is because sunlight reflected from Earth shines onto the nighttime part of the Moon, in the same way moonlight lights Earth at night. This light from Earth is called "earthshine."

▼ Earthshine on the Moon

Moon myths

The ancient Romans called the Moon "Luna," the name of their Moon goddess. Another name for Luna was Diana. The ancient Greeks had a Moon goddess called Selene.

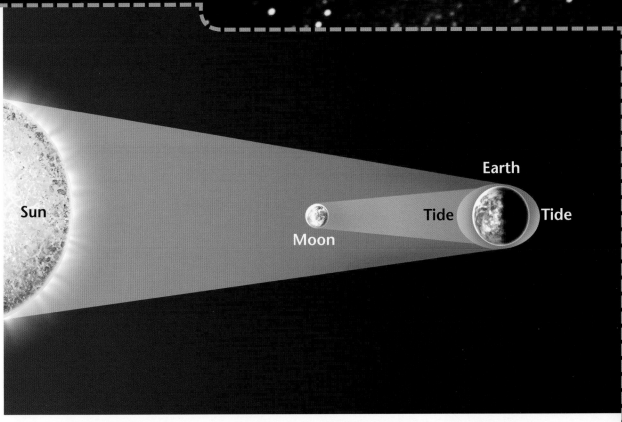

Sun

Moon

Earth

Tide

Tide

▲ At full moon and new moon, when the Earth, Moon, and Sun are in a line, the tide is even higher than normal. The Sun and Moon's gravities work together to pull on the oceans more.

Tides

Earth's oceans rise and fall twice a day. These movements are known as "high tide" and "low tide." Tides are mainly caused by the gravity of the Moon pulling on the oceans.

As Earth spins on its axis, its water bulges towards the Moon, giving a high tide. At the same time, there is a high tide on the other side of Earth. The bulge is actually a little behind the position of the Moon, because it takes some time for the water to react. Between high tides there is a low tide. The tides in any place occur about 50 minutes later each day. This is because the Moon is slowly orbiting Earth.

Lunar Eclipses

Sometimes, when there is a full moon, the Sun, Earth, and Moon line up exactly. Then Earth casts its shadow on the Moon, which turns a soft red-brown color. Lunar eclipses can be seen from anywhere on Earth, as long as the Moon is in the sky when the eclipse occurs.

When the Moon is totally covered with Earth's shadow, it is called a total lunar eclipse. This can last for more than an hour. If the Moon is partly in shadow, it is called a partial lunar eclipse.

Moon

Earth

Sun

Ancient Greek astronomers figured out that Earth is round when they saw the curved shadow of Earth on the Moon.

▲ The cause of a lunar eclipse

▶ The progress of an eclipse of the Moon

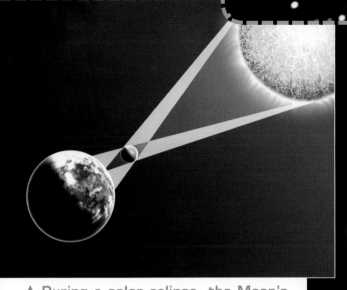

▲ During a solar eclipse, the Moon's shadow darkens part of the Earth.

It is dangerous to look at a solar eclipse because the Sun burns our eyes.

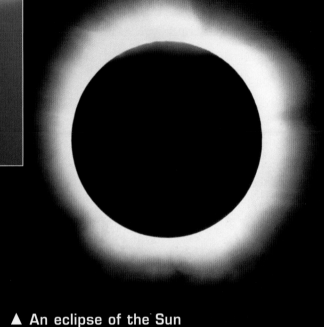

▲ An eclipse of the Sun

Solar Eclipses

Sometimes, when there is a new moon, the Sun, Moon, and Earth line up exactly. Then the Moon blocks out the Sun's light, and casts a shadow on Earth. The sky turns dark and the stars come out. This is called a total solar eclipse. If the Moon partly covers the Sun, the sky does not darken. This is called a partial solar eclipse.

The Moon and the Sun happen to be the same size in the sky. This means that in a total eclipse, the Moon covers the Sun exactly. The gases around the Sun show up against the dark sky. Each total solar eclipse can be observed from only a small part of Earth, and usually only lasts for about 2 minutes.

Exploring the Moon

The Moon was first explored by astronomers using telescopes. It was not until the late 1950s that people used spacecraft to learn more about the Moon.

In 1609, Galileo used a telescope he had made to discover details of the Moon's surface. He named the flat gray plains "*maria*," which means "seas." One sea is called a "*mare*."

The space probe *Luna 2* crash-landed on the Moon in 1959. The next month, *Luna 3* took the first picture of the far side of the Moon. *Luna 9* was the first space probe to have a soft landing on the Moon, in 1966. It sent the first pictures of the Moon's surface back to Earth.

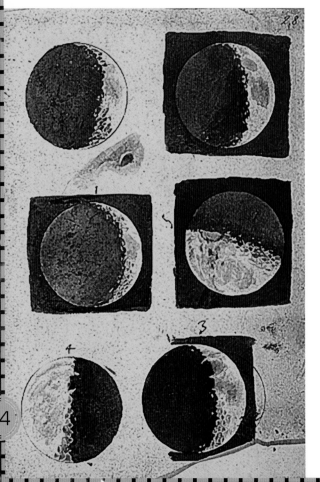

◀ Galileo's first drawings of the Moon, as observed through a telescope

▲ The launch of *Apollo 11*

Apollo Missions

The Apollo program was designed to send astronauts to explore the Moon. Each Apollo journey was called a mission. There were 11 Apollo missions which flew astronauts into space. Six of these missions landed on the Moon.

Apollo 7 and *Apollo 9* flew astronauts around Earth to test the spacecraft and equipment. *Apollo 8* and *Apollo 10* went around the Moon without landing. The *Apollo 11, 12, 14, 15, 16,* and *17* missions all landed astronauts on the Moon. *Apollo 13* was meant to land on the Moon, but there was an explosion in an oxygen tank and the astronauts had to come back to Earth. They barely made it.

Astronauts on the Moon

The *Apollo 11* mission was the first to take astronauts onto the Moon. The landing craft, known as a "lunar module," was called the *Eagle*. The *Eagle* landed on July 20, 1969. It only had 30 seconds worth of fuel left.

The astronaut Neil Armstrong was the first person to step onto the Moon, 6 hours after landing. He was joined by another astronaut, Edwin Aldrin. A third astronaut, Michael Collins, stayed in the spacecraft orbiting the Moon. This spacecraft would later take the astronauts back to Earth.

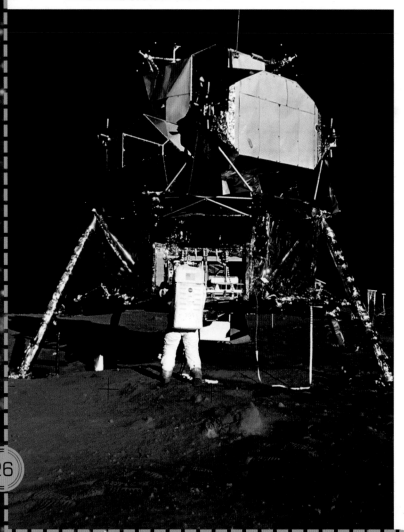

Astronauts in the first three missions onto the Moon all landed on seas. They stayed close to their lunar modules, and did not explore very far.

◄ *Apollo 11* astronauts landed on the Sea of Tranquility.

Landing sites of Apollo missions

Apollo 11	Sea of Tranquillity
Apollo 12	Ocean of Storms
Apollo 14	Crater Fra Mauro
Apollo 15	Hadley Rille
Apollo 16	near Crater Descartes
Apollo 17	near Crater Littrow

▲ Lunar rover on the *Apollo 17* mission in the Taurus Mountains

Astronauts on the *Apollo 15*, *16*, and *17* missions took lunar rovers with them. These electric-powered buggies took astronauts exploring further distances than before. These three missions all landed in highland areas of the Moon.

Astronauts on all missions collected rocks and soils and brought them back to Earth. They brought back about 840 pounds (380 kilograms) of rocks and soil altogether. These samples have shown scientists much about the Moon's make-up and history. Astronauts set up instruments for measuring moonquakes on four places on the Moon. These help scientists figure out what is inside the Moon.

More Discoveries

The space probe *Clementine* visited the Moon in 1994. It orbited the Moon and took three million photographs of its surface. The pictures have been made into the first complete maps of the Moon. *Clementine* also had an instrument on board which detected the heights of mountains. As *Clementine* orbited the Moon, it discovered there was probably some water ice deep in some craters near the Moon's south pole.

The space probe *Lunar Prospector* arrived at the Moon in 1998. It has also found there is probably water ice on the Moon. The ice may be in craters at both the south pole and the north pole. Craters at the poles are shaded from the Sun.

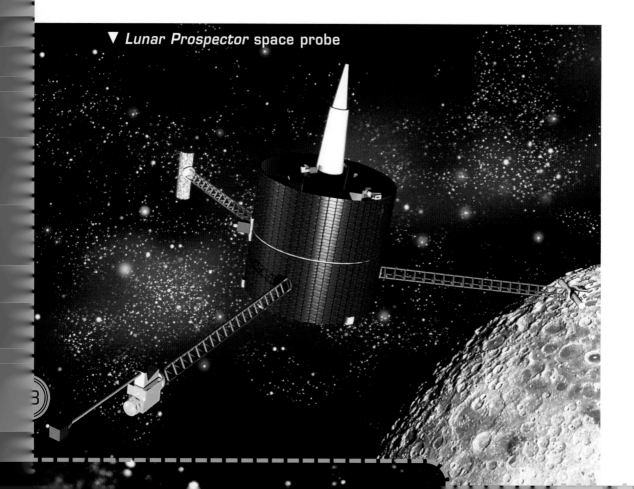

▼ *Lunar Prospector* space probe

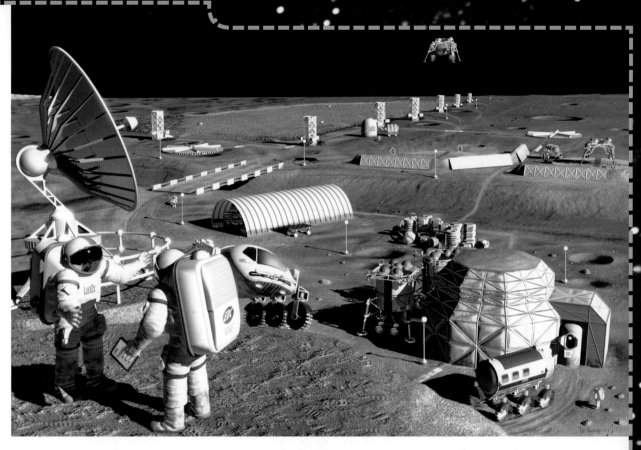

▲ One day, people might live on the Moon.

The Future

There are no plans in the near future to send astronauts back to the Moon, but space probes visiting the Moon continue to gather more information and make more detailed maps of the Moon. They keep looking for ice on the Moon, and they measure the Moon's **magnetism** and gravity. Space probes are looking at the shapes of surface rocks and at what they are made of. They study space around the Moon. The effect the **solar wind** has on the Moon is also studied.

   The information gathered about the Moon could help scientists plan a base on the Moon where instruments could be set up, and, perhaps, where people could live.

Moon Fact Summary

Distance from Earth (average)	238,700 miles (384,400 kilometers)
Diameter (at equator)	2,159 miles (3,476 kilometers)
Mass	0.0123 times Earth's mass
Density	3.34 times the density of water
Gravity	0.17 times Earth's gravity
Temperature	(day) 225 degrees Fahrenheit (107 degrees Celsius), (night) –243 degrees Fahrenheit (–153 degrees Celsius)
Rotation on axis	27.3 Earth days
Revolution around Earth	27.3 Earth days

Web Sites

www.lpi.usra.edu/expmoon/apollo_landings.html
Apollo missions

www.nineplanets.org/
The eight planets—a tour of the solar system

www.enchantedlearning.com
Enchanted Learning Web site—click on "Astronomy"

stardate.org
Stargazing with the University of Texas McDonald Observatory

Glossary

ancient lived thousands of years ago

astronauts people who travel in space

astronomer person who studies stars, planets, and other bodies in space

atmosphere a layer of gas around a large body in space

axis an imaginary line through the middle of an object, from top to bottom

binoculars an instrument with two eye pieces, for making faraway objects look bigger and more detailed

core the center, or middle part of a solar system body

craters bowl-shaped hollows in the ground

density a measure of how heavy something is for its size

diameter the distance across

gas a substance in which the particles are far apart, not solid or liquid

gravity a force which pulls one body towards another body

hemisphere half of a globe

lava hot liquid rock

magnetism a force a magnet has, to attract similar bodies

mantle the middle layer, underneath the crust

mass a measure of how much substance is in something

molten melted into a liquid

moons natural bodies which circle around planets or other bodies

orbits travels on a path around another body in space

planet a large, round body which circles the Sun, and does not share its orbit with other bodies (except its moons)

poles the top and bottom of a globe

revolve travels around another body

solar wind a stream of particles coming from the Sun

space probe an unmanned spacecraft

star a huge ball of glowing gas in space

telescope instrument for making objects look bigger and more detailed

trans-Neptunian objects small solar system bodies which orbit the Sun farther out than Neptune, on average

volcanic caused by volcanoes

volcanoes holes in the ground through which lava flows

Index